Gwyneth Rees is half Welsh and half English and grew up in Scotland. She went to Glasgow University and qualified as a doctor in 1990. She is a child and adolescent psychiatrist but has now stopped practising so that she can write full-time. She is the author of the bestselling Fairies series (*Fairy Dust, Fairy Treasure, Fairy Dreams, Fairy Gold, Fairy Rescue, Fairy Secrets*), *The Magical Book of Fairy Fun, Cosmo and the Magic Sneeze* and *Cosmo and the Great Witch Escape*, and *Mermaid Magic,* as well as several books for older readers. She lives in London with her family.

Visit www.gwynethrees.com

Amanda Li is a children's writer who lives in London. She and her daughters, Izzy and Millie, love books about fairies and are hoping they'll soon find a real one living at the bottom of the garden.

Gwyneth Rees

more magical fairy fun

Compiled by Amanda Li

Illustrated by Emily Bannister

MACMILLAN CHILDREN'S BOOKS

First published 2006 by Macmillan Children's Books
a division of Macmillan Publishers Limited
20 New Wharf Road, London N1 9RR
Basingstoke and Oxford
Associated companies throughout the world
www.panmacmillan.com

ISBN 978-0-330-45202-1

A CIP catalogue record for this book is available from
the British Library.

Typeset by Nigel Hazle
Printed and bound in the UK by CPI Mackays, Chatham ME5 8TD

Contents

From Gwyneth Rees

There's even more fun to be had with the fairies
in my second magical book of fairy fun. All the
fairies you like are back again – Snowdrop, Ruby,
Sapphire, Emerald, Star, Moonbeam, Bonnie,
Goldie, Precious and Cammie (the wee man).
And there are some new fairies too! There's
Poppy – who is a very special fairy because she
only has one wing – and her friends Daisy and
Primrose, who get kidnapped in *Fairy Rescue*.
And there are the fairies from *Fairy Secrets*
– Myfanwy and Bronwen, who are Welsh valley
fairies that ride a flying Welsh pony and whose
job it is to make old toys come to life.

If you've read *Fairy Rescue* you'll know that from
time to time all the different kinds of fairies in
my books – flower fairies, tooth fairies, book
fairies and dream fairies – like to get together
and have fun, so that's what they do in my fairy
fun book. The only trouble is that my fairy
queens – Queen Mae, Queen Amethyst, Queen
Celeste, Queen Eldora, Queen Flora and Queen

1

Lily of the Valley – sometimes argue when they get together, so I hope they won't be arguing too much about the puzzles in this book!

I often get asked if I have a *favourite* fairy and I always find that a really difficult question to answer because I actually have quite a few favourites! Snowdrop from *Fairy Dust* is special because she was the first fairy I ever wrote about, and Cammie the wee man (who doesn't really like to be called a fairy) is special too because he's based on an imaginary friend I had when I was little. Ruby from *Fairy Treasure* is also special because she's the only fairy I've named after a real person – a very special little girl who is the daughter of my oldest friend. (Ruby's mum and I have been friends since we were six and we used to like playing pretend games together – including ones about fairies!) But I also loved writing about Precious from *Fairy Gold* because she was my first naughty fairy, and Star and Moonbeam are definitely my dreamiest fairies, which makes them extra special too. So you can see why it's very hard to pick just one favourite!

If you've read my books then you might have your own favourite fairy already – or if not then maybe you'll have picked one by the time you've finished all the activities in this fairy fun book. In any case I'm sure you're going to have a great time trying out all the fairy puzzles and quizzes and other fun things to do – which are especially made for children who are as mad about fairies as I am!

3

Cast of Fairies

Ruby

Snowdrop

Queen Amethyst

Queen Mae

Queen Celeste

Goldie

Bonnie

Sapphire

Cammie the
wee man

Emerald

Moonbeam

Buttercup

Myfanwy and Bronwen

Queen Flora

Queen Eldora

Queen Lily
of the Valley

Precious

Poppy

Star

Opal

Daisy and Primrose

5

Fairy Types

In Gwyneth Rees's fairy books, there are four types of fairy. Do you know what they are? Match the missing letters to the right word and write them in the spaces.

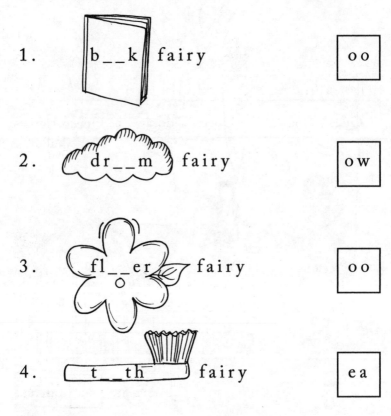

1. b _ _ k   fairy   oo

2. dr _ _ m   fairy   o w

3. fl _ _ er   fairy   oo

4. t _ th   fairy   e a

The answers are on page 137.

Find the Forest Fairies

Maddie is in the forest looking for a fairy party. How many fairies can you see? Count them and write the number in the box.

There are ☐ fairies.

The answer is on page 137.

Fairy Word Grid

Read the clues opposite and write the answers in the grid above.

The word that will appear downwards in the box is the name of a type of fairy who might appear if you sleep in a magic bed!

Clues:

1. A liquid that appears on plants in the mornings. It is also one of the fairies' favourite drinks.

2. A creature that can be very helpful to the fairies, especially when it lets a fairy sit on its back while it flies.

3. A bad person who wanted to capture a fairy would probably use a _____.

4. This would be the best place to find a book fairy.

5. The name of a flower fairy and also the name of a pretty yellow flower that loves the sun.

The answers are on page 138.

Fairy Talk

Which of these characters from Gwyneth Rees's books would say the words in each of the speech bubbles? Match the bubbles to the right character.

A — I rule the fairies in Dreamland.

B — I've lost my wee sock!'

C — If only I could meet a real fairy!

D — Any more teeth to collect?

E — I only have one wing.

The answers are on page 138.

Fairy Ball Wordsearch

The fairies are busy getting ready for a ball. They need lots of things to help them look their best. Can you find the eight words below in the word search opposite? They may be up, down, across or diagonal, either forwards or backwards.

DRESS
SHOES
TIARA
JEWELLERY
MIRROR
BRUSH
RIBBON
PERFUME

12

T	U	W	O	N	T	I	A	R	A
A	S	E	B	S	M	H	J	I	F
N	H	R	I	B	B	O	N	A	P
W	O	E	D	O	D	A	S	E	O
J	E	W	E	L	L	E	R	Y	J
E	S	I	F	H	I	F	O	N	R
T	I	G	S	H	U	C	T	D	E
J	N	U	S	M	I	R	R	O	R
A	R	I	E	J	B	B	D	G	E
B	O	W	S	S	E	R	D	A	M

The answers are on page 138.

13

Count the Jewels

Look at this glittering fairy jewellery! Can you carefully count the jewels to complete the sums? Write your answers in the diamonds.

1 ◯ + ◯ = ◇

2 ◯ + ◯ = ◇

3 ◯ + ◯ + ◯ = ◇

4 ◯ + ◯ + ◯ = ◇

The answers are on page 139.

14

Fairy Dreams

What do you think this little fairy is dreaming about? Draw your idea in the cloud above her head.

Fairy Name Wordsnake

Look at the list of fairy names below. Can you trace the words in the grid opposite using a pencil? They go in one continuous line, snaking up and down, backwards and forwards, but never diagonally.

POPPY

PRIMROSE

DAISY

OPAL

SNOWDROP

RUBY

BONNIE

STAR

GOLDIE

START

P	O	I	D	L
P	P	E	G	O
Y	P	R	R	A
D	E	I	S	T
A	S	M	E	I
I	O	R	N	N
S	N	O	O	B
Y	S	W	B	Y
O	L	D	U	R
P	A	R	O	P

The answer is on page 139.

17

Four Fairy Queens

Each of these fairies is Queen of a different group of fairies. Do you know which? Look at each Queen and draw a line to match her to the correct crown.

2 Queen Amethyst

1 Queen Mae

A

Queen of the tooth fairies

B

Queen of the dream fairies

18

3 Queen Celeste

4 Queen Eldora

C
Queen of the flower fairies

D
Queen of the book fairies

The answers are on page 139.

Colouring Fun 1

Colour in this picture of Maddie and her dog, Milo. Why not draw some pretty patterns on Maddie's T-shirt and leggings?

Dot to Dot 1

Wow! The fairies have seen something beautiful in the sky. Can you join the dots to find out what it is?

The answer is on page 140.

21

Fairy Rhymes 1

Can you complete each of these fairy rhymes with one word?

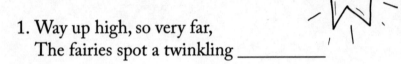

1. Way up high, so very far,
   The fairies spot a twinkling _____

2. To find a fairy, take a look,
   Inside a magic entry _____

3. Good old Poppy! Have you heard?
   She's flying on a helpful _____

4. Oh, look at all the pretty things!
   Tiny fairies, each with _____

5. A fairy picnic – now let's think
   First a sandwich, then a _____

6. Feeling sleepy? Lay your
   head, upon this magic
   fairy _____

The answers are on page 140.

23

Toy Crossword

24

Across

2. This toy goes chuff, chuff, chuffing along on a track.
4. This toy is an animal that swings from branch to branch and loves bananas. It can also be a bit cheeky sometimes!

Down

1. This is a kind of puzzle made from lots of different pieces, which fit together to make a picture.
2. A lovely soft bear that's nice to cuddle.
3. This toy has hair and eyes, and loves to be dressed up in pretty clothes!

The answers are on page 140.

Dotty Drawing

Colour in the shapes that have a dot in them to find a creature that likes humans and sometimes helps fairies.

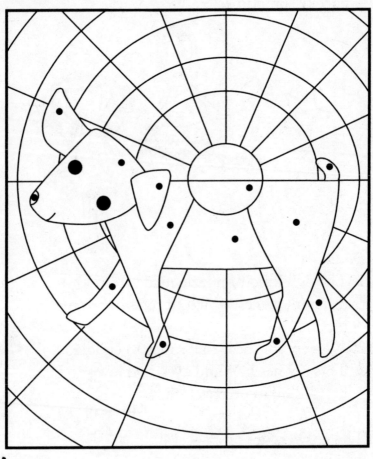

Queen Mae Mix-up

Can you rearrange the mixed-up letters to make
words? Then draw lines to match the words to the
correct parts of Queen Mae.

dawn
_ _ _ _

sniwg
_ _ _ _ _

wrocn
_ _ _ _

ihar
_ _ _ _

sedrs
_ _ _ _ _

The answers are on page 140.

Fruity Fairy Treats

All fairies like eating fruit – and they absolutely
love chocolate! Make these delicious fruity treats
using both their favourite foods.

You will need:
A 115 g (4oz) bar of milk or white chocolate

*A selection of washed fruits: grapes, strawberries and
satsumas (divided into segments)*

A saucepan

*A glass or ceramic bowl that will
fit on top of the saucepan*

A spoon

A piece of greaseproof paper or tinfoil

A grown-up to help

How to make:

1. Fill the saucepan halfway with water and heat on the hob until the water is hot and steaming. **Important!:** Make sure a grown-up does this part as hot water can be very dangerous.

2. Break the chocolate up into small pieces and put them into the bowl.

3. Ask your grown-up helper to place the bowl on top of the saucepan and stir the chocolate gently until it has melted.

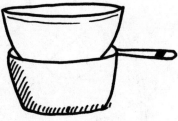

4. Now for the fun bit! Put the bowl of chocolate on a table. Take a piece of fruit and dip it into the chocolate, then lay it on the greaseproof paper or foil. Dip all your fruits like this – why not dip some all over and some just halfway up?

5. You will need to wait 1–2 hours for the chocolate to set. Put the fruits (still on the paper) into the fridge to speed up the process.

6. Once they are set, peel the fruits from the paper and arrange beautifully on a plate. You now have a platter of treats fit for a fairy! Mmmm.

Fairy Picnic Trail

Star, Moonbeam and Twinkle are meeting in the woods for a picnic. Each fairy has brought something delicious to eat. Can you find out what it is by following their trails?

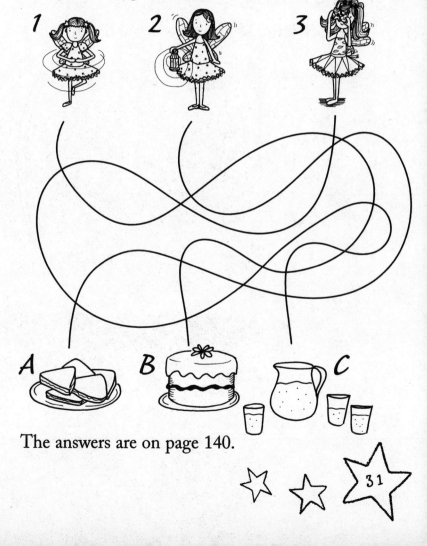

The answers are on page 140.

A Letter From the Fairies

Fairies Bronwen and Myfanwy have sent you a secret message – but it's in code!

Can you work out what they're saying by using the picture code below?

Write each letter in the space as you find it.

_ _ _ _

_ _ _ _ _

_ _ _

_ _ _ _ _ _ _ _ ?

The answer is on page 141.

Fairy Food Sequence

Look at the rows of fairy food below. Can you see a pattern? Draw the last object in each sequence in the box.

The answers are on page 141.

35

Draw a Fairy Picnic

There's nothing the fairies like more than a delicious picnic! Can you create a yummy feast for the fairies? Draw all your ideas for fairy food on to the picnic cloth.

36

Fairy Food Wordsnake

Mmm! The fairies are packing a hamper of delicious food for a fairy picnic. Can you trace the words in the grid opposite, using a pencil? They go in one continuous line, snaking up and down, backwards and forwards, but never diagonally.

JUICE
BERRIES
SANDWICH
BISCUIT
SWEETS
CHOCOLATE
CAKE
LEMONADE
CRISPS

START

J	U	I	S	P	S
B	E	C	I	R	C
E	S	S	A	D	E
R	E	D	N	A	N
R	I	W	I	M	O
I	B	H	C	E	L
S	C	U	E	C	E
S	T	I	T	A	K
W	T	S	A	L	O
E	E	C	H	O	C

The answer is on page 141.

39

Spot the Difference 1

Look closely at the two pictures below. They look similar, but there are seven differences in the second picture. Can you circle the differences?

The answer is on page 142.

41

Colouring Fun 2

Wouldn't you love to share your breakfast with a fairy? Colour in this picture of Maddie and Poppy eating toast and jam.

True or False

How much do you know about fairies? Read the four sentences below and decide if they are true or false, then tick the box.

1. A human cannot shrink down to the size of a fairy. ☐ True ☐ False

2. Fairies are always girls. ☐ True ☐ False

3. Fairies love chocolate. ☐ True ☐ False

4. If a fairy has only one wing, she cannot fly. ☐ True ☐ False

The answers are on page 142.

43

Copy and Colour 1

Can you copy this picture of Maddie, from *Fairy Rescue*, square by square? Then colour her in.

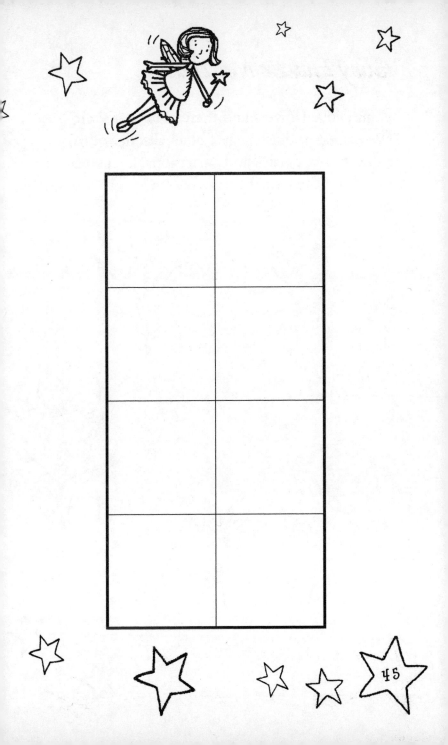

Fairy Flower Matching

Fairies love flowers and there are six of their favourites on these pages: bluebells, daffodils, roses, tulips, daisies and carnations. Can you match up the pairs by drawing lines? Then colour them in.

Fairy Fun 1

What do fairies say when they are
introduced to each other?
'Fairy nice to meet you!'

What do you get if you cross a
wise old fairy with a fish?
A fairy codmother.

What do you get if you cross a
fairy with a jack-in-the-box?
A flapjack.

Knock knock.
Who's there?
Wand.
Wand who?
Wand-er why fairies are so
hard to spot?

Tricky Toothpaste Maze

This little tooth fairy needs some toothpaste for her tooth brushing. Can you follow the toothpaste trail to the tube of toothpaste? Draw a pencil line to reach it.

Toothpaste

The answer is on page 143.

Fairy Shadow Search

One of the fairy's spells has gone wrong and five fairies have lost their shadows. Can you help them by drawing a line to the right shadow?

50

The answers are on page 143.

Make a Tooth Fairy Box

Make this lovely box to put your tooth in the next time one falls out. You might find a nice surprise inside the box in the morning too!

You will need:
An empty matchbox
A piece of paper, coloured or white
Scissors
Glue
Cotton wool or a cosmetic pad
Pens to colour
Small stickers if you have them

How to make the box:

1. Cut a strip of paper that will fit lengthways around your matchbox. Don't worry if it is too wide as you can trim it to fit later on.

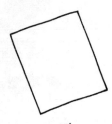

2. Glue the paper all around your matchbox so that it is completely covered (apart from the two ends). Make sure the ends of the paper are stuck down well.

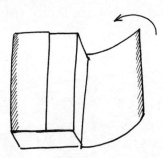

3. Take the cotton wool or cosmetic pad and press it into the empty sliding box part of the matchbox. This is where your tooth will go.

4. Decorate your box. Use pens, stickers or copy/ trace one of the pictures shown to go on the front of the box. Don't use glitter or sparkly bits as these might come off when you put the box under your pillow.

5. You now have your own box for the tooth fairy. When a tooth falls out, place it inside the box and put the box under your pillow when you go to bed. Take a look inside the box in the morning and, if you are lucky, the tooth fairy might have left you a coin!

Ideas for box pictures:

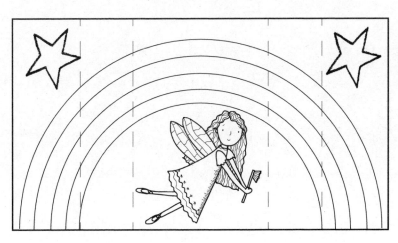

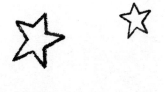

55

A Letter From the Tooth Fairies

The tooth fairies have sent you a secret message – but it's in code!

Can you work out what they're saying by using the picture code below?

Write each letter in the space as you find it.

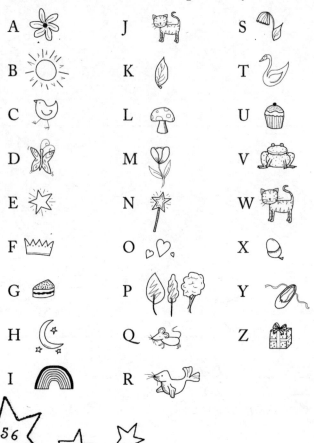

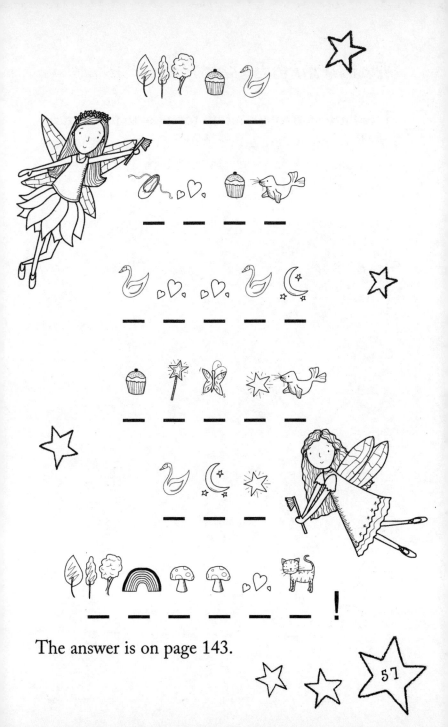

The answer is on page 143.

Tooth Fairy Teaser

The fairies are meeting up for a party tonight. All kinds of fairies are going, but can you spot which ones are tooth fairies? Count them and write the number in the box.

There are ☐ tooth fairies

The answer is on page 143.

The answer is on page 143.

Fairy Tip Remember, tooth fairies carry toothbrushes for their wands!

Colour by Numbers

Fairies Poppy and Opal are having a little rest. Can you colour them in using the numbers as your guide?

1. Black
2. Red
3. Yellow
4. Pale blue
5. Green
6. Pink

A Magic Toy Spell

Myfanwy is sprinkling her magic fairy dust on some of the toys in the toy museum to make them come alive. If you had some fairy dust, which of your toys would you sprinkle it on? Would you like one of your favourite dolls to come to life or perhaps a soft toy like a teddy or a rabbit?

The toy that I would like to come alive is my

_____

_____

Bits About Books

How much do you know about book fairies?
Here are some facts about them:

 Book fairies visit our world through magic books in libraries, called entry books.

 You can identify an entry book because it is covered in sparkly fairy dust.

 Queen Amethyst is Queen of the book fairies. She wears a waistband made from a velvet bookmark and a crown made of gold letters of the alphabet.

 Book fairies love reading! Do you like reading? Write about a book that you enjoyed reading on the opposite page.

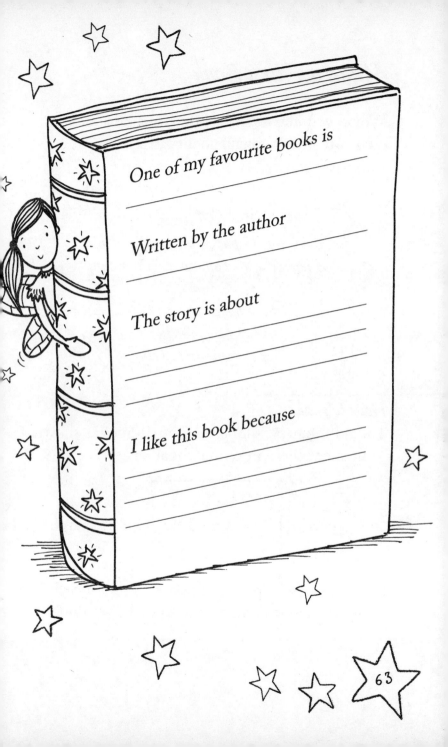

One of my favourite books is

Written by the author

The story is about

I like this book because

63

Make a Fairy Book

Would you like to know how to make your very own cute little book all about fairies? Well, here's how to do it.

You will need:

A piece of A4 paper, coloured or white
A length of ribbon, about 35 cm long
Scissors
Pens and coloured pencils or felt tips
A hole punch
A grown-up to help

How to make:

1. Fold the paper along the dotted lines as shown, then cut them into four equal pieces.

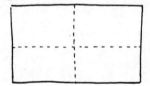

2. Place the four pieces of paper on top of each other, then fold them over to make your book.

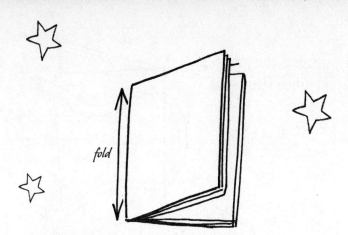

fold

3. Ask a grown-up to help with the next bit. Using the hole punch, carefully punch two holes along the spine of your book – this is the part where the book folds. Be careful not to punch the holes too close to the edge.

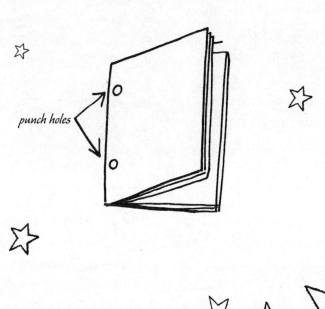

punch holes

4. Thread the ribbon through the holes and tie in a bow at the front of the book. This will be your cover.

tie in a bow

6. Your fairy book is ready for all your ideas! Give the book a title and draw a picture of a lovely fairy on the front cover. Write one thing you know about fairies on every page and illustrate it with pictures. When it's finished why not leave it on your shelf for the book fairies to read – they're sure to love it!

Dot to Dot 2

Join the dots to find which creature Poppy and Maddie are taking a ride on.

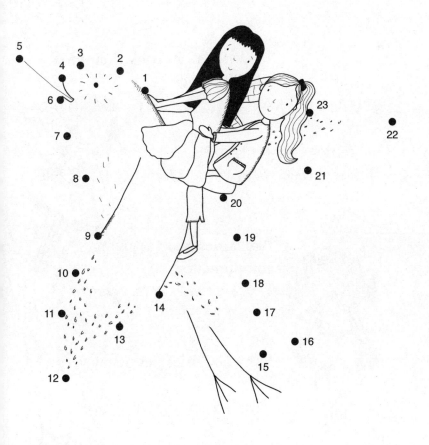

The answer is on page 144.

Fairy Fun 2

What do fairies use to make bread?
Elf-raising flour.

How do fairies cook their food?
In a flying pan.

Do fairies ever get cross?
Well, sometimes they get into a flap.

Are fairies good at giving compliments?
Yes, they flatter as they flutter.

Why do fairies never stay very long?
They like making flying visits.

Draw a Fairy Face

Can you finish the picture by drawing eyes, nose, a mouth and some beautiful fairy hair?

Why not add some sparkly hair-clips or perhaps a lovely tiara?

69

Accessories Wordsearch

Here are eight of the fairies' favourite accessories.
Look at the pictures, then find and circle
the words in the square opposite. The words
are arranged upwards, downwards, across or
diagonally.

B	R	A	C	E	L	E	T	E	B
W	A	T	D	C	R	F	U	E	H
K	Y	G	L	A	S	M	C	I	W
R	O	E	U	G	P	A	R	K	L
E	U	S	O	D	L	Y	O	D	T
C	P	H	T	K	E	G	W	P	I
J	H	O	C	A	N	H	N	S	A
N	M	E	W	I	J	B	Q	E	R
O	N	S	R	Q	T	I	K	F	A
A	D	F	R	N	W	A	N	D	M

The answers are on page 144.

11

Party Paths

These three fairies are on their way to a fairy party. Can you follow their paths and find out which fairy will pick up the most flowers on the way?

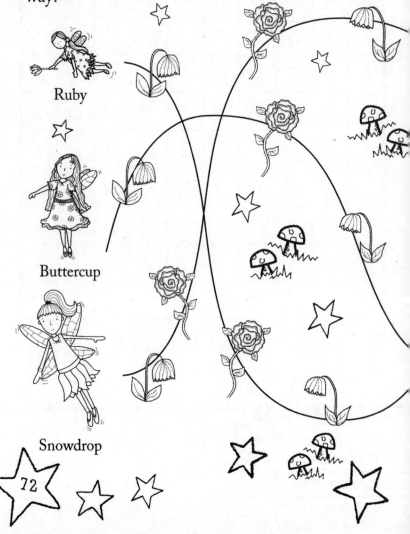

Ruby

Buttercup

Snowdrop

72

The fairy who picked up
the most flowers for the
party is _____

The answer is on page 144.

73

Copy and Colour 2

Copy this picture of Poppy the fairy, square by square. Then colour her in.

Fairy Odd One Out

Look carefully at the fairies below. Can you circle the one fairy in each column that is not the same as the first?

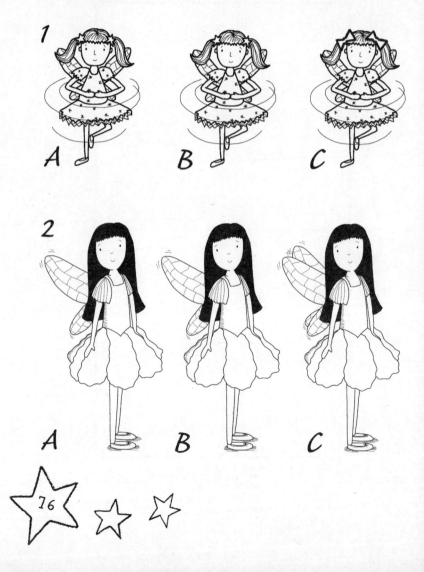

1

A

B

C

2

A

B

C

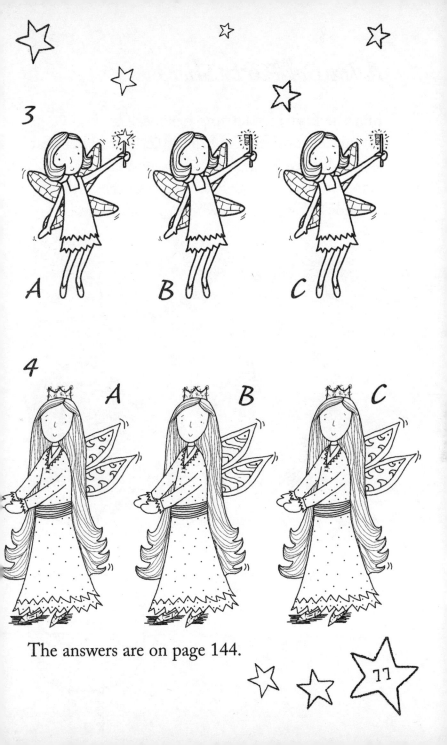

3

A   B   C

4

A   B   C

The answers are on page 144.

A Pair of Party Shoes

Star the fairy is practising her twirls and pirouettes for the fairy ball. But to dance her best she really needs a pair of pretty new party shoes. Can you find her a pair amongst all these mixed-up shoes? Circle them when you find them.

Design a Dress

The fairy dressmakers are busy making new dresses for the fairies for a party tonight. Can you help them? Bronwen needs a new dress and she'd love something with a beautiful pattern on it. Can you draw her a lovely dress below?

Fairy Forest Finds

There are lots of things to see in the fairy forest. How many things begin with the letter f? Count them and write the number in the box.

There are ☐ things beginning with 'f'.

The answer is on page 145.

Party Mix-up

The fairies have invited some of their human friends to their special party. Can you spot which of the partygoers are fairies and which are girls? Count them up and write the number in the box.

There are ☐ fairies.

There are ☐ girls.

The answers are on page 145.

83

Colour Queen Flora

Maddie is amazed when she meets Queen Flora for the first time! Read the description below and colour in the picture of Queen Flora.

☆ ☆ ☆

66 The fairy was surrounded by a rainbow-coloured glow, and as she came closer Maddie saw that she was dressed in a magnificent multicoloured petal dress. She had beautiful sparkling wings and violet-petal slippers, and on her head was a crown made from forest flowers. Her delicate shawl was woven from the finest spider's-web thread, which had been coated in morning dew to make it glisten. 'I am Queen Flora – queen of the flower fairies,' she said in a sweet, clear voice. 99

Make a Fairy Favour

Fairies love parties and presents and they sometimes take little gifts called fairy favours home with them. Would you like to make one?

You will need:
A piece of paper
A piece of thin card (coloured or white)
Scissors
Colouring pens
A gift for inside – stickers, pressed flowers or anything small and flat would be ideal.

How to make:
1. Trace the flower shape opposite on to a piece of paper and cut it out. This is your template.

86

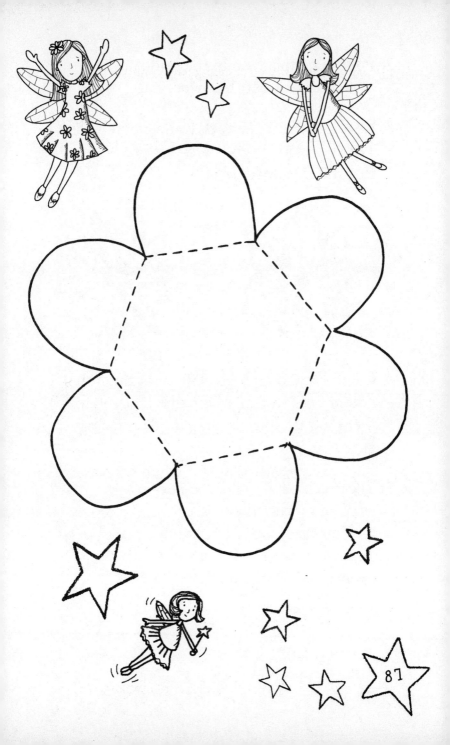

2. Put the template on to the card and trace around it. Cut out the shape.

3. Decorate the shape with your coloured pens. Try drawing flowers, stars, patterns or anything that the fairies would like.

4. Carefully fold each petal inwards along the dotted lines shown. Make sure that you fold them so that your decorated side is facing outwards.

5. Tuck each petal under the next petal and secure the box by tucking the last petal right under. You will now be able to gently open and close the box.

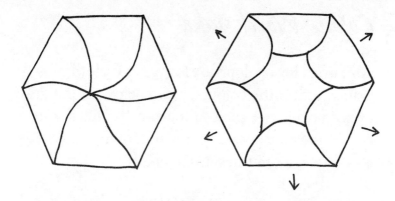

6. Insert your gift into the box. If you don't have anything small and flat, why not write a little note from the fairies and put it inside? A sprinkling of sequins or coloured shapes will finish it off beautifully.

7. Give your fairy favour to your best friend and see her smile!

Colour Wordsnake

All fairies love colourful flowers and clothes.
Can you find the colours, listed below, in the grid
opposite? Use a pencil to trace the words in one
continuous line, snaking up and down, backwards
and forwards, but never diagonally.

YELLOW

RED

BLUE

GREEN

PURPLE

PINK

ORANGE

BROWN

BLACK

SILVER

START

Y	E	L	L	O
B	D	E	R	W
L	U	E	R	E
E	R	G	L	V
E	N	P	I	S
E	L	U	C	K
P	P	R	A	L
I	N	K	N	B
A	R	O	W	O
N	G	E	B	R

The answer is on page 146.

Colour Mix-up

The fairies have lost two letters from each of their colours. Can you draw a line between each colour word and the missing letters?

p _ _ k

g r _ _ n

p _ _ p l e

b l _ _

y e l _ _ w

b r _ _ n

l o

u e

o w

u r

i n

e e

The answers are on page 146.

Rainbow Colouring

All the fairies gather around in excitement whenever a beautiful rainbow appears. Did you know that there are seven colours in the rainbow? Can you fill in the missing colours below, then colour the rainbow in?

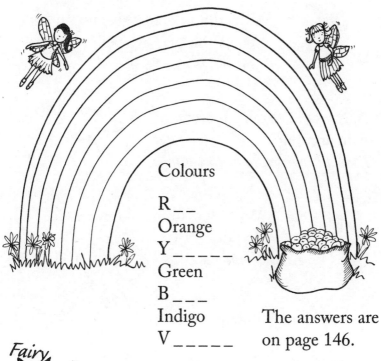

Colours

R _ _
Orange
Y _ _ _ _ _
Green
B _ _ _
Indigo
V _ _ _ _ _

The answers are on page 146.

Fairy Tip

Indigo is a cross between blue and violet. If you can't find the exact colour, try dark blue instead.

93

Fairy Fun 3

How do you know if a fairy had
been working her magic on the
weather?
You'll see lots of sunny spells.

Why did the fairy give up on her
pencil-sharpening spell?
She couldn't see the point.

Why were the fairy football
team arguing?
They all wanted to be the winger.

What sort of computers
do fairies use?
Flaptops.

On which day do fairies buy
their wands?
On Wandsday, of course!

Best Friends

In *Fairy Treasure* Connie really misses her best friend after she and her family move to Canada. But she gets a chance to see her again when the book fairies use their special magic!

What would you miss about your best friend if she wasn't around? Write about your friend in the space below.

☆ Her jokes?

Her hugs? ☆

Her company?

Her kindness? ☆

☆ Her lovely smile? ☆

Her great games?

☆

My best friend's name is _____.
She has _____ hair and _____ eyes.
She likes _____.
She doesn't like _____.
If she wasn't around, I would really miss her

_____.

Animal Shadow Match

Six of the fairies' favourite animals have lost their shadows. Can you help find them? Draw lines between the animal and the correct shadow.

1

2

3

4

5

6

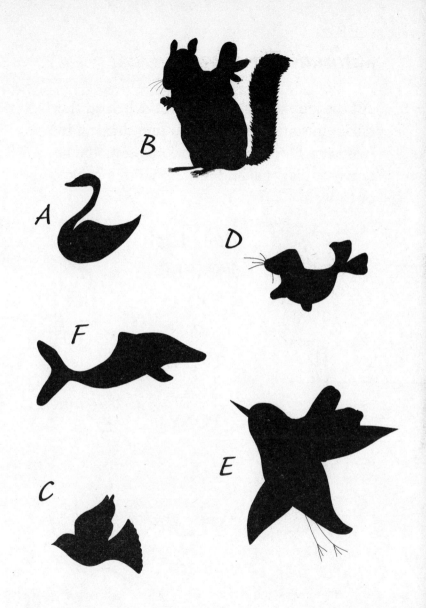

B

A

D

F

E

C

The answers are on page 146.

Animal Wordsearch

All the animals listed below have helped the
fairies in some way. Can you find them in the
wordsearch opposite? The words could be up,
down or diagonal and may be written backwards
or forwards.

DOLPHIN

SQUIRREL

DOG

SWAN

DOVE

SEAL

PONY

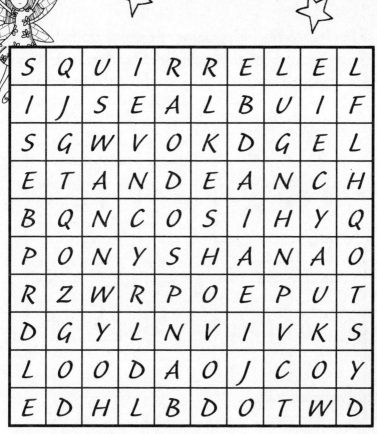

S	Q	U	I	R	R	E	L	E	L
I	J	S	E	A	L	B	U	I	F
S	G	W	V	O	K	D	G	E	L
E	T	A	N	D	E	A	N	C	H
B	Q	N	C	O	S	I	H	Y	Q
P	O	N	Y	S	H	A	N	A	O
R	Z	W	R	P	O	E	P	U	T
D	G	Y	L	N	V	I	V	K	S
L	O	O	D	A	O	J	C	O	Y
E	D	H	L	B	D	O	T	W	D

The answers are on page 147.

99

Find Henrietta Maze

Ellie has to find Henrietta, the china doll, if she is going to save the toy museum. Can you help her? Use a pencil to find your way through the maze.

The answer is on page 147.

100

Dot to Dot 3

Join the dots to find out which animal Poppy is riding on.

The answer is on page 148.

Butterfly Patterns

Butterflies are one of the fairies' favourite creatures. Can you create a beautiful design on this butterfly's wings? Try spirals, stars, spots and dots, zig-zags and hearts. Then colour the butterfly in.

Find the Fairy Name

This pretty little fairy comes from Wales and has a lovely name. Can you find out what it is? Look carefully at the pictures and write the first letter of each picture's name in the box below.

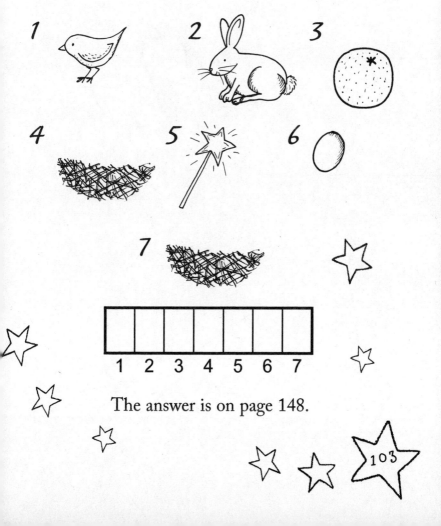

| | | | | | | |
|1|2|3|4|5|6|7|

The answer is on page 148.

103

Spot the Difference 2

Whee! Poppy and Maddie are getting a lift from
a friendly bird. Look at the two pictures below
– they may look similar but the second picture has
eight differences. Can you draw a circle around
each of them?

The answers are on page 148.

Fairy Crossword

How much do you know about fairies? Solve the clues to complete the crossword opposite.

Down

1. A fairy uses her wand to make a magic _____.
3. Fairies use these to make lovely skirts. They drop down from flowers.
5. The name of a fairy, and also the name of a jewel.

Across

2. To meet a dream fairy, you need to sleep in a magic _____.
3. The Queen of the fairies lives in a _____.
4. A tooth fairy uses this as a wand.

The answers are on page 149.

A Pair of Primroses

Primrose squeals with delight as she slides down a ray of sunlight! Can you complete both pictures of Primrose by copying the missing parts from the picture opposite? Then colour them in.

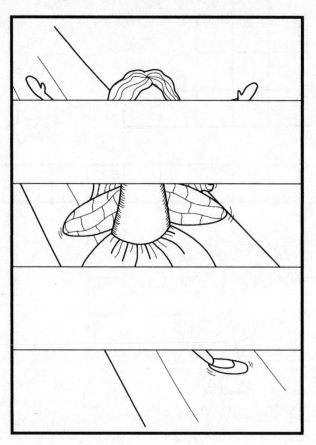

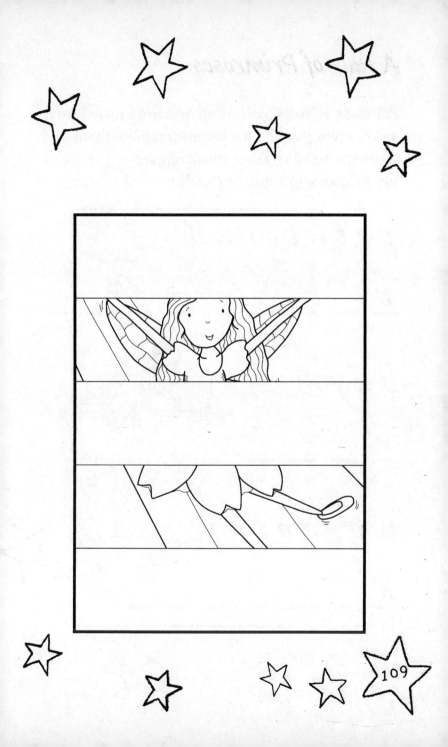

Fairy Name Mix-up

All these fairies have had their names mixed up in a scrambling spell. Can you unscramble them and write the names? They are all named after flowers or types of jewels.

petutcrub

b _ _ _ _ _ _ _ _

buyr

r _ _ _

wosdornp

s _ _ _ _ _ _ _

Fairy Tip Cross each letter out as you use it. Use a pencil and a rubber in case you make a mistake.

l̸oap

o _ _ _

pyoppp̸

p̸ _ _ _ _

rimpseor

p̸ _ _ _ _ _ _

The answers are on page 149.

111

Odd One Out

Look carefully at the pictures below. Can you circle the one picture in each column that is not the same as the others?

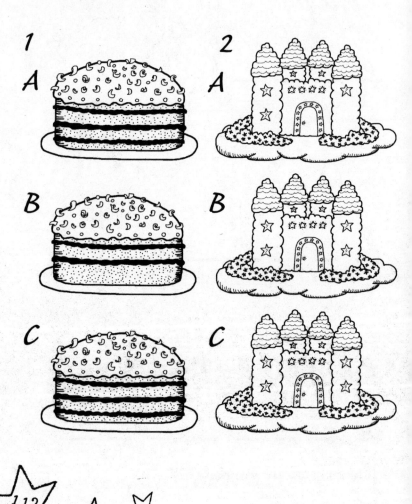

1

A

B

C

2

A

B

C

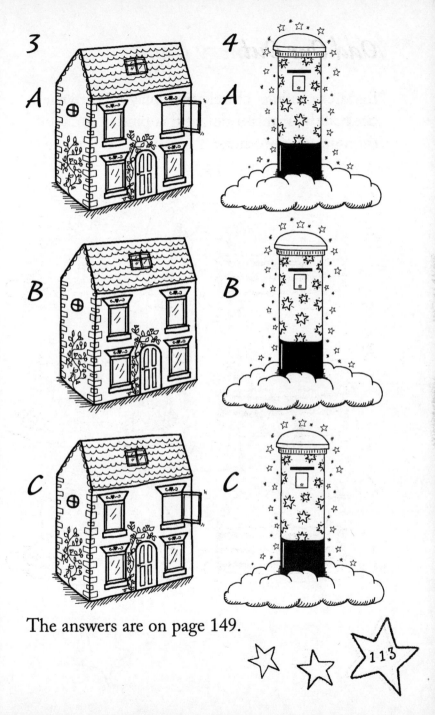

The answers are on page 149.

Maddie's Memory Game

Maddie is having a lovely time playing with these cute baby squirrels! Look at this picture for a few minutes, then cover it up and see if you can answer the questions opposite.

114

1. How many squirrels are in the picture?

_____

2. Is Maddie wearing trousers or a skirt?

_____

3. How many squirrels are eating nuts?

_____

4. Is there a squirrel in Maddie's hand?

_____

5. There are two squirrels on Maddie's lap.

☐ True ☐ False

6. Maddie has got her hair in two bunches.

☐ True ☐ False

7. There is a fairy just behind Maddie.

☐ True ☐ False

The answers are on page 149.

115

A Crown for a Queen

Can you design a beautiful new crown of flowers for the Queen of the Welsh fairies? Queen Lily would also like a lovely new necklace and some earrings. A bracelet or bangle would be nice too!

Cage Maze

Oh no! Daisy and Primrose have been kidnapped and they are locked up in a cage. Can you help them escape? Use a pencil to find a way through the maze.

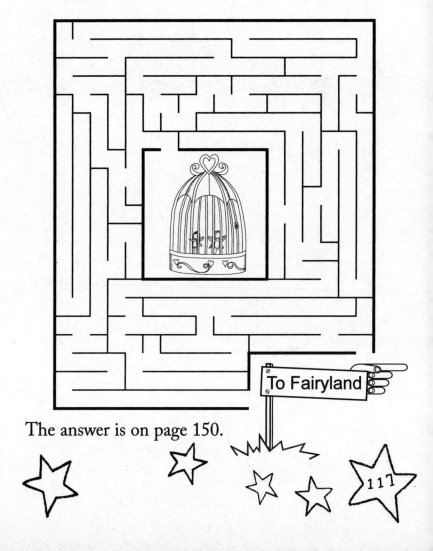

To Fairyland

The answer is on page 150.

Living in the Clouds

Dream fairies live in fairy cloud houses. Look carefully at all these cloud houses. Only two of them are identical. Can you find them?

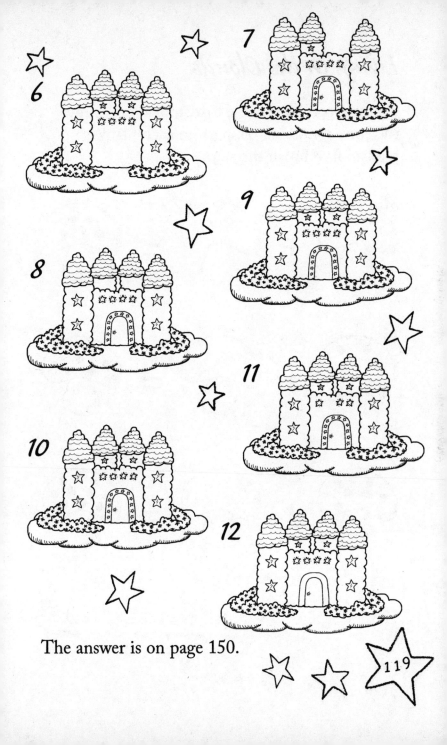

The answer is on page 150.

Tricky Toadstools

Can you complete these toadstool sums? Draw
the correct number of spots on each blank
toadstool to finish the sum.

A + =

B + =

C + =

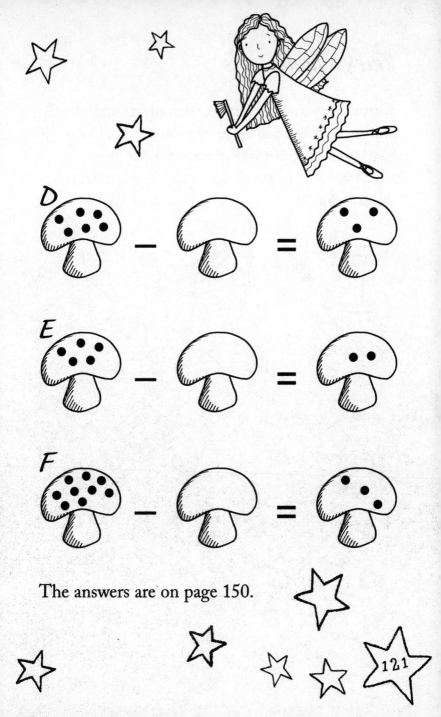

The answers are on page 150.

Fairy Finds

At the fairy lost-property office there are lots of objects that belong to the fairies. But six things have been brought here that are *not* associated with fairies. Can you find them? Circle each of the six objects.

The answers are on page 151.

Count and Colour

It's the middle of the night and Maddie and her mum have gone to the woods to find the fairies. How many of the objects on the page below can you see in the big picture? Count the objects, write the numbers and then colour the picture in.

The answers are on page 151.

125

Girls' Shadow Search

Maddie, Connie and Evie are looking for their shadows. Can you help them? Draw lines to match the right girl to her shadow.

The answers are on page 152.

Dot to Dot 4

Join the dots to find a creature that Horace
Hatter used to collect.

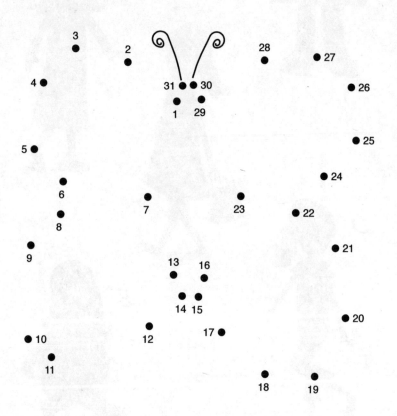

The answer is on page 152.

Colouring Fun 3

Colour in the picture of Maddie and Queen Flora.

Fairy Rhymes 2

Can you complete each of these fairy rhymes with one word?

1. Fairies always take great care
To brush their lovely, shining _____

2. Whenever fairies get the chance
They love to play and sing and _____

3. This dream fairy is very proud
To live in a house made from a _____

4. Cakes and chocolates,
   what a treat,
   To have delicious
   things to _____

5. This little fairy has lost
   her shoe.
   Have you seen it?
   Its colour is _____

6. To make a spell
   a fairy must
   Sprinkle some magic
   fairy _____

The answers are on page 152.

Colour Change Spell

The fairies are using their magic to change the colours of their dresses. Can you help them? Read what they are saying and colour them in.

I'd like a yellow dress with a big pink flower on the front. And pale blue wings!

Fairy Quiz

How much do you know about the fairies that
live in Gwyneth Rees's fantastic stories? Find out
in our fun quiz!

1. Can you name the four different types of fairies
   that appear in Gwyneth Rees's books?

2. What is different about Poppy from all the
   other fairies?

3. What are baby fairies made from? (tick box)
   - [ ] Bundles of joy
   - [ ] Bags of happiness
   - [ ] Boxes of love

4. What colour is fairy
   Emerald's dress?

5. Who is Queen of the tooth fairies? (tick box)

☐ Queen Amethyst
☐ Queen Eldora
☐ Queen Celeste

6. In *Fairy Treasure*, Ruby the book fairy is looking for a lost piece of jewellery. What is it? (tick box)

☐ A ring
☐ A necklace
☐ A bracelet

7. In *Fairy Secrets*, four toys come to life in the toy museum. There is a Welsh doll, a china doll, a toy soldier and one other toy. Can you remember what it is?

8. Poppy the fairy often hitches a ride on the back of a helpful animal. Can you name one of the creatures that gives her a lift?

The answers are on page 152.

Answers

Page 6 – Fairy Types
1. book, 2. dream, 3. flower, 4. tooth

Page 7 – Find the Forest Fairies
There are 10 fairies.

Page 8 – Fairy Word Grid

	1	D	E	W			
2	B	I	R	D			
	3	N	E	T			
4	L	I	B	R	A	R	Y
5	P	R	I	M	R	O	S	E

Page 10 – Fairy Talk
1 – D, 2 – C, 3 – A, 4 – B, 5 – E

Page 12 – Fairy Ball Wordsearch

T	U	W	O	N	T	I	A	R	A
A	S	E	B	S	M	H	J	I	F
N	H	R	I	B	B	O	N	A	P
W	O	E	D	O	D	A	S	E	O
J	E	W	E	L	L	E	R	Y	J
E	S	I	F	H	I	F	O	N	R
T	I	G	S	H	U	C	T	D	E
J	N	U	S	M	I	R	R	O	R
A	R	I	E	J	B	B	D	G	E
B	O	W	S	S	E	R	D	A	M

138

Page 16 – Fairy Name Wordsnake

START

P	O	I	D	L
P	P	E	G	O
Y	P	R	R	A
D	E	I	S	T
A	S	M	E	I
I	O	R	N	N
S	N	O	O	B
Y	S	W	B	Y
O	L	D	U	R
P	A	R	O	P

Page 18 – Four Fairy Queens
1 – C, 2 – D, 3 – B, 4 – A

139

Page 21 – Dot to Dot 1
A shooting star

Page 22 – Fairy Rhymes 1
1. star, 2. book, 3. bird, 4. wings, 5. drink,
6. bed

Page 24 – Toy Crossword

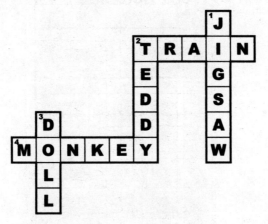

Page 27 – Queen Mae Mix-up
wings, wand, crown, hair, dress

Page 31 – Fairy Picnic Trail
1 – B, 2 – A, 3 – C

Page 32 – A Letter From the Fairies
HAVE YOU GOT ANY CHOCOLATE?

Page 34 – Fairy Food Sequence

1. 2. 3. 4.

Page 38 – Fairy Food Wordsnake

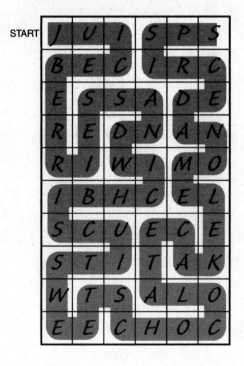

START

Page 40 – Spot the Difference 1

Page 43 – True or False

1. False – the fairies' shrinking spell definitely works on humans!
2. False – Cammie McPherson in *Fairy Dust* is a little man and boy fairies also exist.
3. True.
4. True – Poppy in *Fairy Rescue* has only one wing and she cannot fly (until she gets a second wing near the end of the story).

Page 49 – Tricky Toothpaste Maze

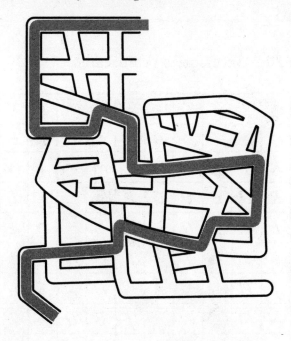

Page 50 – Fairy Shadow Search
1 – C, 2 – E, 3 – D, 4 – A, 5 – B

Page 56 – A Letter From the Tooth Fairies
PUT YOUR TOOTH UNDER THE
PILLOW!

Page 58 – Tooth Fairy Teaser
There are 11 tooth fairies.

Page 67 – Dot to Dot 2
A bird

Page 70 – Accessories Wordsearch

B	R	A	C	E	L	E	T	E	B
W	A	T	D	C	R	F	U	E	H
K	Y	G	L	A	S	M	C	I	W
R	O	E	U	G	P	A	R	K	L
E	U	S	O	D	L	Y	O	D	T
C	P	H	T	K	E	G	W	P	I
J	H	O	C	A	N	H	N	S	A
N	M	E	W	I	J	B	Q	E	R
O	N	S	R	Q	T	I	K	F	A
A	D	F	R	N	W	A	N	D	M

Page 72 – Party Paths
Snowdrop with 7 flowers

Page 76 – Fairy Odd One Out
1 – C, 2 – C, 3 – A, 4 – B

144

Page 80 – Fairy Forest Finds
There are 8 things beginning with 'f'.

Page 82 – Party Mix-up
There are 7 fairies.
There are 7 girls.

Page 90 – Colour Wordsnake

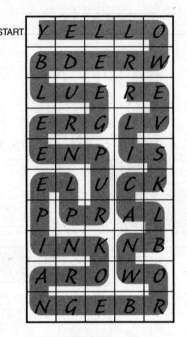

START

Y	E	L	L	O
B	D	E	R	W
L	U	E		R	E
E	R	G	L	V
E	N	P	I	S
E	L	U	C	K
P	P	R	A	L
I	N	K	N	B
A	R	O	W	O
N	G	E	B	R

Page 92 – Colour Mix-up
pink, green, purple, blue, yellow, brown

Page 93 – Rainbow Colouring
red, yellow, blue, violet

Page 96 – Animal Shadow Match
1 – E, 2 – F, 3 – D, 4 – C, 5 – A, 6 – B

146

Page 98 – Animal Wordsearch

S	Q	U	I	R	R	E	L	E	L
I	J	S	E	A	L	B	U	I	F
S	G	W	V	O	K	D	G	E	L
E	T	A	N	D	E	A	N	C	H
B	Q	N	C	O	S	I	H	Y	Q
P	O	N	Y	S	H	A	N	A	O
R	Z	W	R	P	O	E	P	U	T
D	G	Y	L	N	V	I	V	K	S
L	O	O	D	A	O	J	C	O	Y
E	B	H	L	B	D	O	T	W	D

Page 100 – Find Henrietta Maze

147

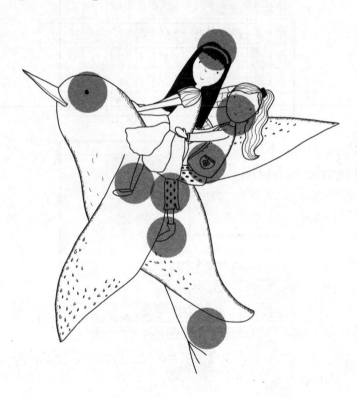

Page 106 – Fairy Crossword

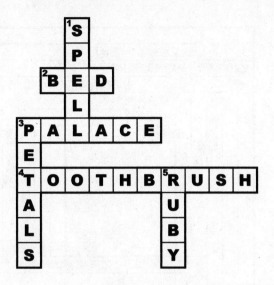

Page 110 – Fairy Name Mix-up
Buttercup, Ruby, Snowdrop, Opal, Poppy, Primrose

Page 112 – Odd One Out
1 – B, 2 – A, 3 – B, 4 – C

Page 114 – Maddie's Memory Game
1. 4, 2. trousers, 3. 1, 4. no, 5. True, 6. False, 7. False

Page 117 – Cage Maze

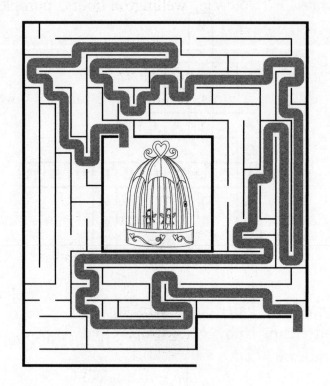

Page 118 – Living in the Clouds
2 and 10 are the same.

Page 120 – Trick Toadstools
A – 2, B – 4, C – 3, D – 3, E – 3, F – 6

Page 122 – Fairy Finds
witch's hat, bicycle, wellington boots, pumpkin, spider, mittens

Page 124 – Count and Colour
4 squirrels, 2 birds, 3 lanterns, 1 fairy, 8 flowers

Page 126 – Girls' Shadow Search
1 – E, 2 – D, 3 – A, 4 – C, 5 – B

Page 128 – Dot to Dot 4
A butterfly

Page 130 – Fairy Rhymes 2
1. hair, 2. dance, 3. cloud, 4. eat, 5. blue,
6. dust

Page 134 – Fairy Quiz
1. Tooth Fairy, Book Fairy, Dream Fairy, Flower
   Fairy
2. She has only one wing
3. Bundles of joy
4. Green
5. Queen Eldora
6. A ring
7. A teddy bear
8. Squirrel, dog (Milo), bird (Starling)